Let all that you do be done in love.

~ 1 Corinthians 16:14

Wherever you go, go with all your heart. Confucius

Opportunities multiply as they are seized. Sun Tzu

I think; therefore I am. René Descartes

Put your heart, mind, and soul into even your smallest acts. This is the secret of success. Swami Sivananda

Wealth is the product of man's capacity to think. Ayn Rand

Health is the greatest gift, contentment the greatest wealth, faithfulness the best relationship. Buddha

We are what we repeatedly do. Excellence, then, is not an act, but a habit. Aristotle

Never was anything great achieved without danger. Niccolò Machiavelli

Clouds come floating into my life, no longer to carry rain or usher storm, but to add color to my sunset sky.
Rabindranath Tagore

Beauty in things exists in the mind which contemplates them. David Hume

What we think, we become. Buddha

Science is organized knowledge. Wisdom is organized life. Immanuel Kant

What worries you, masters you. John Locke

The things that we love tell us what we are. Thomas Aquinas

I want you to be everything that's you, deep at the center of your being. Confucius

In the middle of difficulty lies opportunity. Albert Einstein

He who believes is strong; he who doubts is weak. Strong convictions precede great actions. Louisa May Alc

All that glitters is not gold. William Shakespeare

No great discovery was ever made without a bold guess. Isaac Newton

The course of true love never did run smooth. William Shakespeare

The question isn't who is going to let me; it's who is going to stop me. Ayn Rand

Difficulties are meant to rouse, not discourage. The human spirit is to grow strong by conflict. William Ellery

I hear and I forget. I see and I remember. I do and I understand. Confucius

Nothing can harm you as much as your own thoughts unguarded. Buddha

Where the willingness is great, the difficulties cannot be great. Niccolò Machiavelli

It is not enough to have a good mind; the main thing is to use it well. René Descartes

Know your enemy and know yourself and you can fight a hundred battles without disaster. Sun Tzu

The whole is more than the sum of its parts. Aristotle

Love takes up where knowledge leaves off. Thomas Aquinas

When I let go of what I am, I become what I might be. Laozi

If you truly loved yourself, you could never hurt another. Buddha

Live your beliefs and you can turn the world around. Henry David Thoreau

There is nothing on this earth more to be prized than true friendship. Thomas Aquinas

Enthusiasm moves the world. Arthur Balfour

It is beyond a doubt that all our knowledge that begins with experience. Immanuel Kant

To the mind that is still, the whole universe surrenders. Lao Tzu

A wise man proportions his belief to the evidence. David Hume

When deeds speak, words are nothing. Pierre-Joseph Proudhon

The reading of all good books is like a conversation with the finest minds of past centuries. René Descartes

No act of kindness, no matter how small, is ever wasted. Aesop

To love means loving the unlovable. To forgive means pardoning the unpardonable. Faith means believing the unbelievable. Hope means hoping when everything seems hopeless. Gilbert K. Chesterton

It is during our darkest moments that we must focus to see the light. Aristotle

I cannot teach anybody anything, I can only make them think. Socrates

Since love grows within you, so beauty grows. For love is the beauty of the soul. Augustinus

Judge of a man by his questions rather than by his answers. Voltaire

The world of reality has its limits; the world of imagination is boundless. Jean-Jacques Rousseau

We know what we are, but know not what we may be.
William Shakespeare

Let your life lightly dance on the edges of Time like dew on the tip of a leaf.
Rabindranath Tagore

All that we are is the result of what we have thought. Buddha

Thousands of candles can be lighted from a single candle, and the life of the candle will not be shortened.
Happiness never decreases by being shared. Buddha

The less men think, the more they talk. Montesquieu

There are two ways of spreading light: to be the candle or the mirror that reflects it.
Edith Wharton

Pleasure in the job puts perfection in the work. Aristotle

Don't judge each day by the harvest you reap but by the seeds that you plant.
Robert Louis Stevenson

Happiness is a butterfly, which when pursued, is always just beyond your grasp, but which, if you will sit down quietly, may alight upon you. Nathaniel Hawthorne

Say not always what you know, but always know what you say. Claudius

There is nothing without a reason. Gottfried Wilhelm Leibniz

The foundation of every state is the education of its youth. Diogenes

It does not matter how slowly you go so long as you do not stop. Confucius

You, yourself, as much as anybody in the entire universe, deserve your love and affection. Buddha

Wise men talk because they have something to say; fools, because they have to say something. Plato

Fear cannot be without hope nor hope without fear. B. Spinoza

Hope is the pillar that holds up the world. Hope is the dream of a waking man. Pliny the Elder

Happiness depends upon ourselves. Aristotle

The man who is swimming against the stream knows the strength of it. Woodrow Wilson

He who knows, does not speak. He who speaks, does not know. Laozi

ook within. Within is the fountain of good, and it will ever bubble up, if thou wilt ever dig. Marcus Aurelius

No man's knowledge here can go beyond his experience. John Locke

Thinking: the talking of the soul with itself.
Plato

Grace is the beauty of form under the influence of freedom. Friedrich Schiller

How glorious a greeting the sun gives the mountains! John Muir

Every man's life is a fairy tale written by God's fingers. Hans Christian Andersen

There is only one good, knowledge, and one evil, ignorance. Socrates

Even if I knew that tomorrow the world would go to pieces, I would still plant my apple tree.
Martin Luther

There is nothing impossible to him who will try.
Alexander the Great

Whenever anyone has offended me, I try to raise my soul so high that the offense cannot reach it.
René Descartes

Noble deeds that are concealed are most esteemed.
Blaise Pascal

Let us read, and let us dance; these two amusements will never do any harm to the world. Voltaire

Happiness resides not in possessions, and not in gold, happiness dwells in the soul.
Democritus

Choose a job you love, and you will never have to work a day in your life. Confucius

Out of difficulties grow miracles.
Jean de la Bruyere

If we did all the things we are capable of, we would literally astound ourselves.
Thomas A. Edison

I came, I saw, I conquered. Julius Caesar

Patience is the companion of wisdom. Augustinus

From a small seed a mighty trunk may grow.
Aeschylus

Look within. Within is the fountain of good, and it will ever bubble up, if thou wilt ever dig.
Marcus Aurelius

Peace comes from within. Do not seek it without. Buddha

Every individual is the architect of his own fortune. Appius Claudius Caecus

The only journey is the one within.
Rainer Maria Rilke

Be kind, for everyone you meet is fighting a hard battle. Plato

What makes the desert beautiful is that somewhere it hides a well.
Antoine de Saint-Exupery

You can discover more about a person in an hour of play than in a year of conversation. Plato

Insults are the arguments employed by those who are in the wrong. Jean-Jacques Rousseau

Live your life as though your every act were to become a universal law. Immanuel Kant

There is nothing either good or bad, but thinking makes it so. William Shakespeare